19.5

HEAR, HEAR!

A Guide to Training a Deaf Dog

By Barry Eaton

"...deafness is often a greater handicap to the deaf dog's owner than to the dog."

William E. Campbell

To Lady

CONTENTS

FOREWORD

I first got to know Barry Eaton as a member of the Association of Pet Dog Trainers, a group dedicated to training dogs and puppies with understanding, modern motivational techniques and a patient love of dogs. Barry is a gentle natured man who had realised long ago that effective communication between our two similar but different species was what dog training was all about. But he is also an engineer by profession, (although dog training is now his full-time interest) and so clearly relishes getting to grips with making things work, especially when they get difficult! In fact, if you had to write an advert for someone to take on the task of developing training techniques for dogs which are disadvantaged by being deaf, then you couldn't find a better qualified person than Barry.

But there's my first mistake, and one that so many people make when they contemplate whether even to keep deaf puppies or dogs alive, let alone think about communicating with them or training them. They're not disadvantaged, they're different! It was Barry who taught me that being deaf isn't such a big deal for a dog, as other senses compensate. With nose on the ground and with bright eyes looking up regularly to scan the world for their human or canine companions, they can acquire the signals of how to co-operate and combine activities to everyone's advantage. Dogs, like every other animal work to gain rewards and being highly social, they want to please their owners. What Barry has done with this pioneering 'Bible' for owners of deaf puppies and dogs, is to show us how to communicate effectively with appropriate signals using hand, face and body postures to enable deaf dogs to learn about our requests and be rewarded for responding correctly. Barry describes which signals might work best for different dogs. The 'Eaton canine sign language' is how I like to think of it; how to put ourselves into a silent world and establish just as good a relationship with a deaf dog as we can with one with normal hearing.

If you can take a slice of Barry's own natural patience from his words in this book, (as he outlines from the start, you'll need some in the beginning with a deaf puppy!), you may end up with an even better relationship than usual because your dog is sure to respond to the understanding and effort Barry encourages you to put in.

What I would like to see for this book is not just that it proves to be the standard work for training a dog which is deaf or hard of hearing, because it will surely become this anyway. What I hope is that every trainer in the world will read it and apply the techniques and understanding so well thought through and practised by Barry Eaton. It can only improve the relationship that every owner can have with their dog, whether it can hear or not.

Dr Peter Neville
Animal Behaviour Therapist
Centre of Applied Pet Ethology
PO Box 18, Tisbury
Wiltshire SP3 6NQ

INTRODUCTION

My wife and I bought Lady in 1988 when she was 8 weeks old. In 2002, 14 years later, she died of cancer. During those 14 years she was exceedingly friendly and playful, adored children, and loved our other two dogs. We enjoyed long walks where she ran and played, came back when I called her and walked quietly on-lead. When she was about two years old, she was surrounded by ten Irish Setters, jumping and bouncing all over her as Setters do. Although they only wanted to play, it obviously frightened her and the experience left its mark. Consequently she was not keen on dogs she didn't know coming too close. Apart from that, she was friendly, lively, as obedient as many dogs we met on our walks and probably more obedient than others. A fairly typical average family pet you may think - except Lady was born deaf.

Despite her disability, there was little Lady didn't do as a pet dog that hearing dogs can. OK, she was a bit slow to realise when visitors arrived because she didn't hear the door bell, and she was usually the last to know that it was meal time as she didn't hear the chink of bowls or rustle of the food bag. But she acted and behaved like any other dog and enjoyed life just as much.

Hereditary or congenital deafness occurs in many breeds of dog but some breeds are more susceptible than others. The ear canal opens when the puppy is about two weeks old but it can be difficult to spot any sign of deafness at that age. Deafness may become noticeable at about five weeks of age if the puppy is slow to respond to sound, or has no response at all. Breeders of dogs prone to deafness should check the litter to avoid the possibility of someone unknowingly being sold a deaf puppy.

Regardless of one's view as to whether deaf puppies should routinely be put to sleep, as many are, the fact remains that as long as deaf puppies continue to be born, there will always be people willing to give them a chance of a normal life. It's these owners and their dogs that need help. With care and patience and the right kind of training, a deaf puppy can enjoy a full life; grow up to be an obedient, well behaved member of our society and a pleasure to own. After all, a dog's lack of hearing is more of a handicap to his owner than to the dog himself.

I have no wish to give the impression that training a deaf puppy is as straight forward as training a hearing puppy (if you can describe training any puppy as straight forward). Obviously it won't be. As an owner of a deaf puppy you will need a far greater degree of patience and perseverance than owners of hearing pups. If you already have another, hearing dog, this will definitely help, as the deaf puppy will watch and learn from him, (bad habits as well as the good ones!). That's not to say that the hearing dog will train the deaf one, relieving you of the job. It doesn't work like that. The emphasis of the training is between the deaf puppy and his owner and there must be a strong bond between them.

I hope this book gives you help and encouragement if you have knowingly or unknowingly taken on a deaf puppy. Where does one start? How does one get their puppy back when it's running off-lead? How does one communicate with the puppy? The questions are seemingly endless and I have tried to answer most of them. The training advice is based on my experiences with Lady and from training and advising other owners of deaf puppies.

The one major quality that is essential to owners of deaf puppies is patience. None of the training exercises will be learnt overnight. Daunting the task may be initially, but given time and imagination, your endeavours will reap their own rewards.

Throughout this book I refer mainly to training a deaf "puppy". Regardless of whether you have a puppy or an adult dog the methods and principles of training are the same.

Good luck.

1 WHY IS MY DOG DEAF?

As a dog trainer, genetics is not my forte! Nevertheless I will try to explain briefly (and simply) why dogs are born deaf.

Deafness is a congenital or hereditary ailment passed from one generation to another. Total deafness can occur in both ears (bilateral) or one ear (unilateral) or as partial deafness in one or both ears. Breeds that are prone to deafness can be tested before mating and puppies can be tested as young 5 or 6 weeks old. (See Chapter 3).

Dr George Strain, Professor of Neuroscience at the School of Veterinary Medicine, Louisiana State University, USA has identified 83 breeds in the US that suffer from congenital deafness to some degree. You can check the full list of breeds on his website. You will find that a few of the breeds are not recognised in the UK but most are! His website is;
www.1su.edu/deafness/VetClinNA.htm

Hereditary deafness is linked to the genes controlling pigmentation of the colour of the coat and the eyes. White, merle and piebald coated dogs may suffer from deafness due to a deficiency of melanocytes, the cells that cause the colour of the skin. Due to the lack of this gene the inner ear cannot develop normally, hence causing deafness. Deafness often occurs in breeds if there is a lack of normal iris pigment resulting in the colour of the eyes being blue.

There are breeds that are not known for a white, merle or piebald coat yet can still be affected by congenital deafness. Dr Strain states, *"In the small number of canine breeds where it is not associated with white pigmentation (Doberman and other dog breeds not carrying piebald or merle genes), deafness results from the type of hair cell loss that is a primary event with unknown cause."*

There are in fact a number of different causes of deafness, which are;

1. **Hereditary deafness** where the genes are passed from one generation to another via either sire or dam, or both

2. **Acquired deafness** which can be attributed to injury, disease, or high doses of certain ototoxic drugs which can damage the cochlea and canals in the inner ear, impairing hearing and balance.

3. **Conductive deafness**, which is due to the interference of sound waves to the inner ear. This may be caused by ear wax or a foreign body in the ear canal, infection of the middle ear or rupture of the ear drum.

4. **Sensorineural deafness**, which is due to damage or defect in any part of the auditory pathway from the cochlea in the inner ear via the auditory nerve to the auditory cortex of the brain.

5. **Congenital deafness** means that deafness is present at birth. The most common form of congenital deafness is that it was inherited from the sire, dam or both parents. Alternatively the puppy may have been born with a problem in the auditory system.

6. **Late onset deafness** which is associated with the onset of old age.

2 REASONS TO PUT THE PUPPY TO SLEEP?

During the time I have spent training and advising owners of deaf dogs, I have heard most of the arguments as to why deaf puppies should be put to sleep. The major arguments are;

- The dog will have a poor quality of life.
- He will be 'uncontrollable' and 'untrainable'.
- He is more likely to cause an accident by running into the road because the owner can't call him back.
- He won't be able to socialise properly with other dogs as he can't hear warning growls.
- He will be aggressive.

Let us look at each of these arguments and put them into perspective.

First of all, the argument that the dog will have a poor quality of life. Does the dog know he's deaf? Of course not. If he was born deaf he won't know life as being any different. What you've never had, you'll never miss, and usually, the dog's other senses will compensate. The quality of a dog's life depends on his good health and how his owner treats him, not on whether he can hear or not.

If a dog, any dog, is not trained properly he is likely to be 'uncontrollable'. If he is trained properly, he will be controllable. People who say a deaf puppy is 'untrainable' are usually those who have had no experience training one and have little imagination of how to go about it. A deaf puppy is trainable if it is approached in the right way.

There has been much talk about the danger of a deaf dog being the cause of traffic accidents because if he runs towards a road, the owner cannot call him back; the inference being that if the

dog could hear, he would stop chasing the cat or rabbit and obediently return to his owner. Now let's get back to the *real* world. How many average pet dog owners could honestly say that their dog would stop chasing another animal and return to his owner when called? How many owners could honestly say that their friendly dog would not run across the road to see another dog or to say 'hello' to somebody on the other side? Not many, I'm sure.

NO dog should be off-lead near a road, regardless as to whether he is deaf or not or how well trained the owner thinks he is. Sensibly, a deaf dog should be on-lead when anywhere near a road. He should also be trained to keep an eye on his owner and to obey a recall signal before being let off the lead (See Chapter 8).

The next argument is that a deaf dog will not be able to socialise with other dogs nor be able to hear any warning growls. Dogs are masters at reading body language. A major part of dog/dog communication is by body language, more so than by the noise it makes. There may be a slight risk that another dog will attack from the rear taking the deaf dog by surprise, but it is a slight risk and no reason to condemn a deaf puppy to death on the off-chance that that situation will occur.

The emphasis with any puppy is to socialise it as early as possible. If the puppy is socialised from an early age he should grow up to be a happy, friendly dog. (See Chapter 3)

There are many reasons why dogs become aggressive. Puppies bred from nervous or aggressive stock, lack of socialisation when a puppy, or a bad experience when still young, to name but three. It doesn't follow therefore, that just because a dog is deaf, he will also be aggressive. Neither does it follow that if a deaf dog is aggressive, the aggression should be attributed to the fact that he is deaf.

In my view, these 'arguments' are just convenient excuses as to why a deaf puppy should be put to sleep, but they can also be attributed to any dog, whether it can hear or not. Instead of thinking and acting negatively, why not get to grips with the problem of training a deaf dog and develop a training programme, just as there is for hearing dogs? Until deafness in puppies is eradicated there will always be people who are willing to give them a chance of a normal life. These puppies and their owners need help just as much as any other dog and owner.

Reasons for Getting a Deaf Puppy

There are probably loads of reasons why people end up with a deaf dog, but in my experience there are two main reasons, both of which can be attributed to human emotions;

The unsuspecting deaf puppy owner. A breeder sells a puppy but unbeknown to the breeder or the new owner, he's deaf Later, the owner's suspect something is not quite right; he's not responding to early training or is slow to respond to sound, and tests show he's either partially or totally deaf. The breeder offers to take him back but only to have him destroyed. By then of course, the owners have become so attached to the new member of their family that the thought of having him destroyed is unthinkable.

Emotional blackmail. A potential owner is 'taken in' by a hard-luck story, something like; 'I have a puppy for sale but he's deaf and if I can't find him a good home he'll have to be put to sleep.' It is surprising how many people fall for that one. I did!

There is in fact a third, but not very common reason why somebody has a deaf dog. A breeder who only breeds an occasional litter may find that one of the puppies is deaf. Not having the heart to have him put to sleep or trust somebody else to bring him up, keeps him.

3 FIRST THING'S FIRST

INFORM THE BREEDER

Breeders of dogs that are susceptible to deafness should check their litters for deafness, but if you are unknowingly sold a puppy that is deaf, you must immediately inform the breeder so the source of deafness can be traced. Even if the puppy is partially deaf, you must inform the breeder who can then take steps to ensure that the sire or dam is not bred from again.

The breeder may offer to take the puppy back, but most will then have him put to sleep. The decision to keep the puppy, or not, is entirely yours. If you decide to keep the puppy, it's not unreasonable to expect a partial refund of the purchase price.

A VISIT TO THE VET

The next thing to do is visit your veterinary surgeon to have him checked out and to start his course of inoculations. Your vet may suggest carrying out some tests to determine if the deafness is hereditary or whether there is a deformity or disease in the ear. While a deformity or disease may be treated and even cured, there is no cure for hereditary or congenital deafness.

You should also discuss with your vet the earliest possible time to have your puppy neutered as this is essential. I realise there are people who still think it "cruel" to neuter a dog, or it's not "macho" to have a castrated dog, but it will be foolhardy to risk the genes for deafness being passed on to other puppies.

TESTING FOR DEAFNESS

Testing for deafness has moved on from the days when a vet stood behind the dog and clapped his hands, and the dog's response, or lack of it, determined whether he was deaf or not. Today puppies can be scientifically tested using sophisticated computer technology. In 1992 a test called a Brainstem Auditory Evoked Response (BAER) was introduced into the UK and this can determine whether your puppy is totally or partially deaf in one or both ears. The test consists of a sound at different levels of decibels being presented to the puppy through headphones. This generates an electrical signal which is recorded and displayed on a computer. The test can identify if there is a problem, the site of any problem, the probable cause and whether treatment is possible. Puppies as young as five weeks old can be tested for deafness. Sensibly, dogs of breeds that are susceptible to deafness should be tested before mating. There are only a few centres who are equipped to carry out these tests, so ask your vet to refer you to your nearest one.

TRAINING CLASSES

Unfortunately, there are some dog clubs that will not accept a deaf puppy into their class. Personally, I think this is a sad reflection of the limited training capabilities of those trainers. Just because your puppy is deaf, there is no reason why he shouldn't go to training classes and join in all the activities.

One piece of advice I give to my clients, even though they are coming to me for one-to-one training, is to enrol in a training class. I sent one of my students with her Dalmatian puppy to an enlightened training class and at the end of the course she gained top marks, something that had never been achieved before by any dog. She then graduated to the more advanced class at the end of which, again achieved top marks.

Despite those clubs that won't allow deaf puppies, there are many good puppy training classes that will. However before enrolling in a class, go and watch a session to see how they operate. If they won't allow you to watch, go somewhere else. Ideally you should find a class specifically for puppies between the ages of about 12 weeks and 24 weeks. There should be a limit on the number of puppies attending to ensure a balance of group activity and individual tuition. An open-door policy could result in chaos and a lot of sitting around waiting to do something. Training methods should be kind and fair, using rewards, like titbits and toys, and positive reinforcement. If you see owners or instructors using choke chains, don't enrol. Talk to the instructors and ask pertinent questions about their experience, qualifications and how they would help you with your deaf puppy.

Training classes whose instructors are members of the Association of Pet Dog Trainers (APDT) are unlikely to turn away a puppy because of his deafness. Appendix I has the contact details of the APDT addresses in the UK and the USA, or ask your local vet who may have the address of your nearest APDT member. The APDT has a strict code of practice that ensures puppies are trained using non-punitive methods.

Unless the instructor has experience of training a deaf puppy, go prepared to do your own thing, but listen to the instructor's advice, particularly regarding any behavioural problems you may be having with your puppy.

EQUIPMENT

No special equipment is required to train your deaf puppy. All that is needed is a leather collar, leather lead, an extendible lead, a long line, a toy and some titbits. When I was training Lady, these basic items of equipment are all I needed. Since then collars that emit a vibration have become commercially available and these may be of benefit for training. I certainly wouldn't put people off trying them but having successfully trained Lady without one as they weren't available then I tend towards caution when advising on their use. In my experience, the main reason most owners want a vibrating collar is to use it as a 'recall' for their dog. The problem with this is that just as hearing dogs can be selectively deaf when called, so deaf dogs may selectively ignore the vibration of the collar should they associate it with the recall.

Initially, the dog needs to be conditioned to the collar so it just gets his attention and he looks to the owner. It's taking the place of saying the dog's name to get his attention. It should not be used in my opinion, as any particular command, least of all the 'recall'.

Being a remote device there's obviously a range involved but what happens when the dog is out of range? There is no training in place that the owner can rely on for the dog to look back at some point to see where the owners are going and what they are doing. Also what happens if the dog goes into a river or lake? The collar is not totally waterproof so it will be ruined.

Care should also be taken when introducing a vibrating collar to an older dog as the new stimulus may cause distress to the dog.

Personally, I don't think there is any substitute for actually training the dog to keep an eye on his owners to see where they are going and what they are doing, all of which is described in my book. However if you feel it may help then by all means try it.

Incidentally, the vibrating collars should not be confused with those that emit an electric shock.

You will note that there is no mention of choke chains, spiked collars or electric collars as these items are simply not required. The misuse of these types of collars can result in severe injury, or even death, to any dog, and under no circumstances should they be used on puppies.

4 SOCIALISATION

An essential part of a dog's education is learning how to cope with everyday life. He must become accustomed to, and behave correctly with, people old and young, male and female, and other animals both within his home environment and in the outside world. This is an extremely important process for any puppy but probably more so with a deaf puppy. You must accustom him to as many different stimuli and different types of people, so he has the attitude of 'seen it, done it, read the book, got the tee shirt' and takes life in his stride.

Socialisation with people should start when the puppy is about 2 weeks old by being picked up and gently handled. If puppies are subjected to mild stress at this age, they are more likely to cope with other stresses later in life. If a puppy has not been socialised with people by the age of 12 weeks, it may have a detrimental effect on his future behaviour. Equally important is the puppy's socialisation with other dogs. A puppy must learn how to behave and interact with other dogs or he may grow up to be fearful of them.

So the responsibility for starting the puppy's socialisation lies with the breeder, and should be continued by the new owner when the puppy goes off to a new home. But having gone to a new home, there is this period of 'solitary confinement' when the puppy is not allowed out because he is waiting for his vaccinations to take effect. This doesn't mean he can't be socialised. Invite friends, relatives and neighbours, including children, round to meet your puppy. Invite men with beards; wearing a uniform or carrying a stick or umbrella; anything that may be slightly unusual.

You can also take your puppy out in the car for short journeys so he gets used to car travel and he can see there is more to his world than the back garden. Carry him out into the street so he can see and smell the outside world.

Some veterinary practices hold 'puppy parties' which is an excellent way for owners to continue the socialisation process. Puppy parties are usually run by a veterinary nurse and consist of a number of puppies who are in the process of having their inoculations. The puppies learn to play and interact with each other while the nurse explains about puppy care and welfare. Later, when the inoculations are complete, you can graduate to a puppy training class, where he can continue with his socialisation and you can practise your training techniques with the distractions of other puppies and their owners.

GROOMING AND HANDLING

Many people groom their dog only when he needs grooming but this may be so infrequent that the dog is not used to it and objects. He may try to bite the brush, or the owner's hand, or he'll squirm around the floor and be a general fidget. The owner ends up fighting the dog to carry out the simplest grooming task - and the dog usually wins. Bearing in mind that you won't be able to use your voice to control your dog, it's better that he becomes used to being groomed from an early age, so when the time comes and he really needs brushing, he's quite happy about it.

Brush your puppy every day whether he needs it or not. Gently groom him for just a few seconds to begin with, after which give him a food treat or play with him so he associates being groomed with something nice. Everybody in the family must groom the puppy including children but only under parental supervision.

There will undoubtedly be occasions when you will need to examine your dog. He may have a lump that needs inspecting, a grass seed stuck in his paw or a tic that needs removing. In any event he will need his claws clipped. Rather than waiting until the situation arises, start to accustom your puppy to being handled. Gently hold each paw in the palm of your hand and run your thumb over the top of the paw. Gently lift each lip in turn so you can inspect his teeth. Look at his eyes, in his ears and under his tail. It is most important that all your actions are gentle so you progress gradually as your puppy becomes more confident with what you are doing. Like grooming, everybody in the family must be able to inspect your puppy including children but only under parental supervision.

Figure 1. Inspect and groom your dog every day

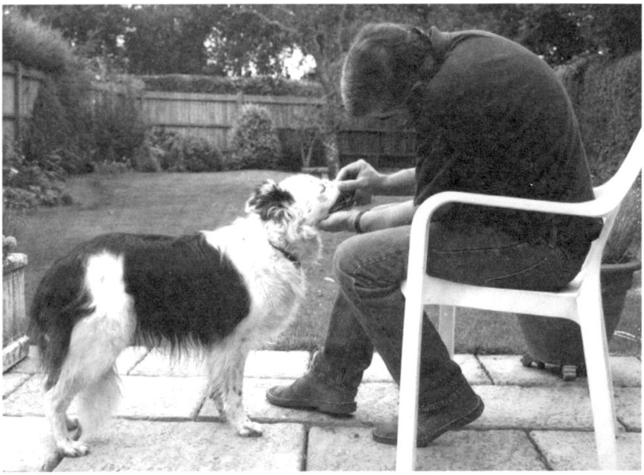

When your puppy is happy about being handled, invite friends and neighbours to have a go, then perhaps the milkman and postman. The more people who can handle your puppy, the more confident he will be. And let's face it there will be occasions when your dog needs to be examined by the vet and this will make his job a lot easier.

During the process of grooming and handling, if your puppy is being tolerant, smile to show him you are pleased with him. If he objects, stop what you are doing, have a blank facial expression and wait for him to settle down before continuing.

5 COMMUNICATIONS

Without the benefit of voice control, you will need to be a little more inventive in how you communicate with your puppy. The three main ways of communicating with a deaf dog are:

- hand signals
- facial expression
- body posture

HAND SIGNALS

Hand signals will be your primary form of communication and they must be clear and exaggerated. As all the family should be involved with training your puppy, you must all agree what hand signals to use before training begins. Keep hand signals consistent. Everybody must use the same signals otherwise you will confuse the puppy and training will take much longer. Don't forget also to think of a way to communicate the equivalent of "good dog", "bad dog" because let's face it, no matter how sweet your puppy is, he's not going to be a perfect angel all the time!

It doesn't matter what hand signals you use to command your dog. The important thing is that he understands them. After all, you don't have to teach a hearing dog to sit by saying 'sit'. You can say 'cabbages' if you like, providing you teach the dog that 'cabbages' means 'sit'. I know of a dog that was taught to sit with the command 'park it'. It works the same way with hand signals.

When training a dog for obedience competition, there is a convention for using a particular hand signal with the spoken command. If you prefer to use those signals, fine. The hand signals I use, which are explained in the book work for me, and Lady understands what I'm asking of her, but they are not written in tablets of stone.

There are a few things to consider before deciding on the signals to use.

- Keep the signals clear and exaggerated. Over the years, some of my signals have become quite subtle as Lady has become more adept in knowing what I'm asking of her but to start with, they were very exaggerated.

- Don't make them complicated. Keep them simple so as not to confuse your puppy.

- Plan ahead for when the puppy is an adult dog and may be some distance from you. For example, a lady told me that she 'called' her deaf puppy by tapping her legs and he responded to it. That might work indoors or in the back garden, but when the dog is in the park, off-lead, some distance away, he's not likely to see a tap on the legs. So the recall signal in particular must be very clear.

- Try to structure your signals so you can reinforce the command through two stages. 'Ask' your dog to do something then, if he doesn't comply, 'tell' him. You must use a firmer series of signals in conjunction with body language and facial expression. With a hearing dog, the owner can use the tone of his voice to enforce the command through those stages if necessary. You don't have that luxury and must therefore be more inventive.

None of the signals, regardless of what it is for, should require you to actually touch the dog.

BODY LANGUAGE/FACIAL EXPRESSIONS.

You can also use body posture and facial expression to convey your pleasure or displeasure. Dogs are masters at reading body language. Much of dog/dog communication is by reading each others body posture and facial expressions, more so than the noise they make. Dogs can detect the most subtle changes in the body posture of their owners even though the owners won't realise it. You must be aware and emphasise the use of your body language and facial expressions to help you communicate with your puppy.

FACIAL EXPRESSION

To help you convey the right message to your puppy, talk to him. All right, so he won't be able to hear you but if you say positive things, it reinforces a positive facial expression and body language, which all goes to help communicate the right message to your puppy. Also - smile. Put on a happy face. If you smile when you are rewarding or praising your puppy, he will learn that a smile means you are pleased with him.

Imagine you've been working hard to train your puppy to lie down and after much perseverance he finally does it. If you just think 'good dog' it is very difficult to convey through facial expression how you really feel. However, if you say 'good dog' and really mean it, your face will automatically brighten, you'll smile and your eyes will light up. Over a period of time, your puppy will understand that a smile means that you are pleased with him as he's done the right thing.

However, if during your training session your puppy refuses to lie down your face must be a total blank so as not to convey any emotion until he achieves what you want from him. Then, with spoken praise, your face brightens up. You must not use a scowl or a harsh facial expression if he does not do what you are asking of him, as this must be reserved exclusively for when your dog has done something wrong and you need to reprimand him. There is no place for reprimands during a training session. If your dog doesn't lay down when you ask him, he probably doesn't understand what you are asking of him and you cannot tell him off for that.

Stand in front of a mirror and practise facial expressions. Happy, delighted, over-the-moon expressions. A totally blank expression. Unhappy, angry, if-looks-could-kill, expressions. All have their uses at the right time.

BODY POSTURE

Body language also plays an important part in communicating with your dog. Crouching down with arms open wide is a wel-coming posture to a puppy. Bending over a puppy is a threatening posture. So take care to combine the right facial expression with the right body posture. For example, bending over and smiling may give conflicting signals.

Figure 2.
Good Dog!

Figure 3.
Bad Dog!

6 ATTENTION!

Being able to get and keep your puppy's attention is essential. If you cannot get his attention you cannot train him. If you have your puppy's attention, he is more likely to stay with you when you are out on a walk, so find what his favourite toy is and use it to your advantage. When you are on a walk, play with the toy with your puppy, then after a few minutes, put it away. When you start to lose his interest, take the toy out again and play with him. This will keep your puppy guessing as to when you will play with him and eventually, he will learn to focus his attention on you – because you are fun to be with. Only use this toy for training or when out on a walk.

Figure 4. Teach your puppy to pay you attention

"But my dog isn't interested in toys", I hear you say. Are you sure? Just because you spent a few pounds at the pet shop on a toy, it doesn't mean your dog is going to like it. Find out what he likes rather than what you want him to like.

If he really isn't interested in anything, here's how to cultivate an interest. Start to play with your puppy without a toy. When he's getting excited, introduce the toy and continue to play with him until he starts to take notice of it. Then stop playing and hide the toy under your sweater or in a paper bag. Tease your puppy by showing him part of the toy and then hiding it away again. By repeating this play scenario, you are continually increasing your puppy's interest in a particular toy and each time you stop playing with it, you leave him wanting to play with it. Later in the book, I explain how I keep Lady's attention using a ball when she is off-lead.

Getting your dog's attention when he is not looking at you requires a little common sense. There are only a limited number of ways to try to get his attention, none of which are guaranteed to work. It's a question of trying them to see which one, if any, is successful. You can try throwing a bean bag or knotted handkerchief into the dog's line of vision. You must be extremely careful not to hit the dog and with this in mind, do not use something that is too heavy.

Try a beam from a torch to get his attention, although you may find that herding breeds are more interested in chasing or herding it. Switch the room light on and off; stamp on the floor, particularly if it's floorboards rather than a concrete floor. If your dog is lying against a chair, hit the chair so the object of his disturbance is the chair, not you.

A very Important point to remember is never get your deaf puppy's attention by physically touching him, particularly if he's asleep or unaware you are in the room. If you touch him and startle him, he could become very nervous and possibly snap. This is where families with young children are most at risk. Accidents will happen. The child may fall on the puppy when he's sleeping or innocently stroke him when he's not looking, making him jump. Therefore great care must be taken when there are young children in the family.

7 PRAISE AND REPRIMAND

It's easy for owners to praise or reprimand a dog that can hear simply by using the tone of their voice. With a deaf dog it is equally important for him to know if he's done right or not. Therefore you will need to have a signal for 'good dog', and 'bad dog'. (See figures 2 and 3).

PRAISE

Praising your puppy for doing something you want him to do is relatively easy but, nevertheless, very important. A very happy, over-the-moon facial expression, a hand signal, perhaps a thumbs-up sign and maybe an affectionate stroke will all convey your pleasure. Also in training, rewards of a food treat or play with his favourite toy will also convey the fact you are happy with him.

REPRIMAND

There will be times when your puppy will get into mischief or do things you don't want him to do, so you need to let him know when he is doing something unacceptable. With a hearing dog, the voice, if used correctly, is usually a sufficient reprimand. However this is not an option open to you, so you need to use an alternative. There are two stages of reprimand;

The warning. You must start to use a hand signal that will warn your puppy that he is doing something you don't want him to do. I use a wagging finger, the way my mum used to admonish me when I was a lad, a serious body posture and stern facial expression, (Figure 5). If you scowl at him and are leaning over him when he is doing something wrong, (which is a threatening

posture to a puppy), he will eventually learn that whatever he is doing is wrong. Lady now knows that a wagging finger means, whatever you are doing, don't!

It is important to precede punishment with a warning signal so he starts to learn what it means. If you do not teach your puppy a warning signal, every time he does something you don't want him to, you will have to resort to punishment, which isn't fair on your puppy. If you are consistent with your approach to praising and reprimanding your puppy he will eventually understand.

The punishment. The punishment is a last resort and should only be used if interrupting the unwanted behaviour and the warning has failed. The most effective punishment is to isolate your puppy from the rest of the family. Remove him to the kitchen, close the door, and leave him for a few minutes. When

Figure 5.
The warning

you let him out, direct his attention on something you DO want him to do, and then praise him for doing it. There is never any reason to physically punish your puppy, regardless of whether he can hear or not. If you use your hand, rolled up newspaper or anything else, you run the risk of your puppy growing up to be hand-shy, nervous and aggressive. Your hand should be something your puppy trusts, not fears.

Never punish or reprimand your puppy for getting something wrong in training. Training must be pleasurable and him so he learns quicker and without fear. There will be times when you need to correct your puppy when he is about to do something unacceptable or potentially hazardous, like chewing electric cables, without actually punishing him. The best way of achieving this is to give him a small fright by directing a squirt of water from a water pistol behind the ear. By the time he looks round to see what it is, you have hidden the water pistol behind your back and have an innocent, "who me?" look on your face, so he doesn't associate the correction as coming from you. This method of correction should not be perceived as a punishment and therefore no warning precedes it. Under no circumstances should the dog see the water pistol otherwise it may turn into a game!

8 PAWS FOR THOUGHT

Before we start looking at the training exercises, just take some time to think about how you will go about it.

COMMITMENT

Are you totally committed? If not, you should be. Training will be time consuming, frustrating and challenging. There are no short cuts, quick fixes or magic formulae, but ultimately it will be exceedingly rewarding.

If you have made the right decision for the right reasons in getting a deaf dog, and that is by carefully thinking about what you are taking on instead of letting your heart rule your head, you **must** be dedicated towards the dog's training because you have taken on that responsibility.

If you have knowingly or unknowingly taken on a deaf dog and have decided to keep him then again you have taken on the responsibility to train the dog so you too **must** be dedicated. Love alone will not train your dog. You **must** be dedicated to training your dog.

You must also have a composed disposition when training. Dogs are masters at reading body language and facial expressions, in fact that's their main way of communicating with each other. So if you come home from work in a bad mood, even though the dog won't hear what a foul mood you are in, he will be able to read your body language, so that is not a good time to start a training session. You have to be relaxed - calm - chilled out!

WHAT AGE?

What age should the puppy be before you start to train him? Once upon a time it was thought that you shouldn't train a dog until he was six months old. Just think how many bad habits he will pick up in that time. The adage 'prevention is better than cure' is as true in dog training as it is in anything else. Also, at six months of age your 'puppy' is no longer a puppy. At this age dogs start to develop sexual maturity; males are capable of mating and bitches come into season for the first time.

It is generally accepted that a dog's behaviour is moulded during the first few weeks of his life, so the more of the right things he learns while still a puppy, the better behaved adult dog you will have. So the best time to start training is the day you get your puppy home - or the day after, and the best time to start training classes is when your puppy has completed his inoculations at about 12 or 13 weeks of age, or earlier if your vet allows.

HOW LONG?

It isn't possible to say how long it will take to train your puppy although it will probably take longer than a hearing puppy as you do not have the benefit of voice control. Puppies will learn at their own pace, which could be a matter of weeks, months or even years depending on the standard you hope to achieve. Some exercises like the 'sit' could be learned quite quickly. Others like 'stay' and 'loose lead walking' may take longer. Be prepared to persevere.

Keep training sessions short, no longer than 3 or 4 minutes, but as often as you can during the day. Also take advantage of opportunities that present themselves. For example if you are in the kitchen waiting for the kettle to boil and your puppy is with you, use the time to practise a few 'sits' and 'downs'. Training sessions should be fun for you and your puppy so don't look on it as a chore. At the end of each session, reward your puppy by playing with him with his favourite toy.

MOTIVATION

Your puppy will learn quicker if he is motivated to do what you are asking, so one of the first things you must do is find out what motivates him. It may be a favourite toy, but most puppies are motivated by food, so find something other than his usual meal-time food to motivate him during your training sessions. If you use food treats you must keep an eye on his weight and make allowances to his daily food intake if necessary. As well as using titbits for rewarding good behaviour, they are also used to lure your puppy into the position you want, e.g. sit, down, stand, 'loose lead walking', etc. Titbits should not be used as sweets for your puppy. They are to be used as a reward and are to be earned.

I use liver cake which I make myself, and find it works wonders. For those of you who are a dab hand in the kitchen, here's the recipe;

1 lb liver, ½ lb plain flour, 1 egg.
Liquidise the liver, mix in the flour and add the egg. A little milk can be added if you wish. Spoon into a lightly greased sponge tin and cook in a moderate oven for about 20 minutes. Cut into small pieces when cool. It can be stored in the freezer and a few pieces taken out to thaw for few minutes and used as required.

Some people consider using titbits as a bribe. I see it as a wage for a job well done. After all, we are not bribed to go to work, but we do get paid. The titbit only becomes a bribe if your puppy won't do what you ask unless he gets a titbit. As you don't want to get your puppy hooked on titbits, as soon as he is consistently doing what you are asking, start to phase them out. Only reward the best response to your hand signal, and then, when he's responding perfectly every time, reward him intermittently so he doesn't know when the reward is coming.

OTHER THINGS TO REMEMBER

Training a hearing puppy can be exceedingly frustrating. Training a deaf puppy will, occasionally, be even more frustrating. When you feel the frustration welling up, stop training. Take a break. Take it out on a pillow - not your puppy. Remember that training should be fun for you and your puppy.

If there are young children in the family, you must explain to them that the puppy cannot hear. This can be very confusing for children to understand but you must take care that they do not startle the puppy when he is not looking or is sleeping, as, like any other dog that is startled, he could snap.

When your puppy does something on his own accord, like walking towards you, do not ignore it or take it for granted. Reinforce his action with your 'recall' hand signal and praise him when he gets to you. Do not be impatient. Build on each success and do not expect too much too soon.

9 TRAINING

The general rule for training puppies is; praise the behaviour you want; ignore the behaviour you don’t want unless it is so bad, in which case, interrupt it. Therefore, when training your puppy, he will either be rewarded for getting it right, or if he doesn’t get it right, there is no reward.

The following training exercises are all hands-of. There is no need to push, pull, squish or squash your puppy into a position. If you are squashing your puppy into a ‘sit’ or ‘down’ for example, you will not be able to reinforce what you are doing with a hand signal.

SIT

Show your puppy you have a food treat and, with your fingers outstretched, place it in the palm of your hand. Then hold it in place by placing your thumb over it, (Figure 6) and turn your hand over so the palm is facing downwards. Place your hand just above the puppy’s nose and move it slightly back over his head. As he looks up towards the treat, his rear end will go down. As soon as he sits, give him the treat, smile and give him a stroke. You will need to repeat this several times until he gets the hang of it. As you begin to phase out the titbits, your outstretched hand, palm downwards, will become your hand signal for ‘sit’, (Figure 7). Don't forget though, you will still need to ‘praise’ your dog every time he sits.

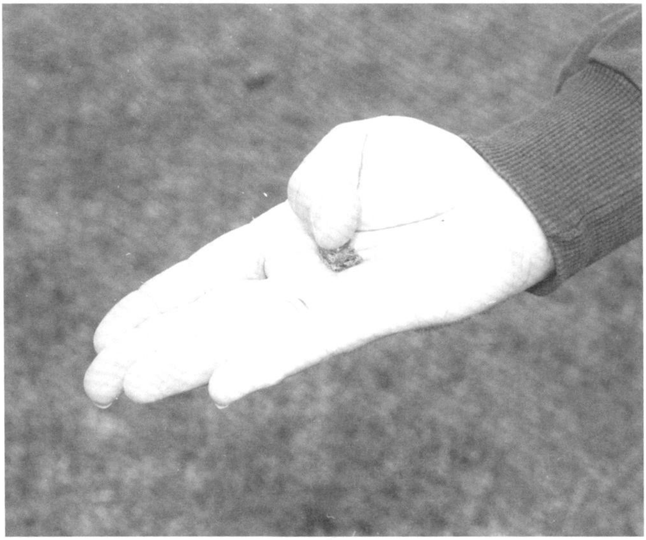

Figure 6. Holding the titbit

Figure 7. Asking your dog to sit

It should not be too long before your puppy starts to understand what your 'sit' signal means but occasionally he may decide to ignore you. So now you start to introduce the next level of command where you don't 'ask' your puppy to sit, you 'tell' him. If he does not respond to the request to sit, with a blank facial expression, use a firm downward 'sit' signal, lean slightly over him and take one step threateningly towards him. (See figure 8). As soon as he sits, smile and reward him. You must not use this level of command until you are sure your puppy understands the 'sit' signal.

Figure 8. Telling your dog to sit

DOWN

It is easier to teach the 'down' when your puppy is in the 'sit' position. Place the titbit between fingers and thumb and lower your hand to the floor between the puppy's front paws and wait! (Figure 9). Given time, your puppy will lower himself to the ground in his attempt to get the treat. As soon as he is lying down, and only when he is lying down, give him the treat, smile and 'praise' him.

You will need lots of patience for this exercise as it generally takes longer for the puppy to understand what he needs to do. While you are waiting for him to lie down, do not move your hand around; keep it still between the front paws. If he stands up instead of lying down, lure him back into a 'sit' and start again. As soon as he is getting the idea, start to phase out the titbit and only reward the best response.

Figure 9. Lure into a 'down'

Once your puppy begins to understand that fingers held on the floor means 'down', you can slowly refine the signal so that ultimately, all you need to do is point to the ground. However, you should not try to refine the signal until your puppy understands that the initial signal means 'down'. Start refining your signal by lowering your hand to within one inch of the ground and when you are getting the desired response, lower it to within two inches of the ground and so on. So gradually you are lowering your hand less and less. My own signal for Lady to lie down is just to point my forefinger downwards, (Figure 10).

Figure 10. Asking your pup to lie down

If you are sure your puppy understands the 'down' signal but chooses to ignore you, you can then move to the higher level of command. With a blank facial expression, use a firm downward 'down' signal, lean slightly over him and take one step threateningly towards him. (See figure 11). As soon as he lies down, smile and reward him. The higher level of command should not be used until your puppy fully understands the 'down' command, but fails to comply.

Figure 11. Telling your pup to lie down

STAND

I'm often asked why someone would want to teach their pet dog to stand if the dog isn't going to participate in obedience competitions. Being able to give a signal to stand will help when grooming, and inspecting your dog for lumps and bumps. When being examined by the veterinarian, they might need the dog to stand particularly when you think about where the thermometer is placed when taking the dog's temperature! So a hand signal for 'stand' can make life a lot easier.

Figure 12. Luring your puppy into a 'stand'

With your puppy in a 'sit' and with the titbit between fingers and thumb, place the titbit in front of his nose and slowly move your hand away from him, keeping it directly in line with his nose. As your puppy gets up to follow your hand, stop taking your hand away and give him the titbit and praise him. Ideally you should be standing for this exercise and your arm outstretched so that when you lure your puppy into a stand, your arm is travelling back to your side, (Figure 12).

Eventually you should end up with a straight arm signal that starts off just in front of you and is then drawn back to end up at your side or just behind you, much like a soldier swinging his arms when marching, (Figure 13).

Figure 13. Final 'stand' signal

GETTING YOUR PUPPY TO COME BACK TO YOU

Probably the most important thing any dog owner wants to teach their dog is for him to come back when called. You have probably noticed that most dogs suffer from selective deafness when it suits them, usually when they are chasing a cat or rabbit, or in the middle of a good game with another dog. The owners stand in the middle of the park calling and calling their dog, getting angrier and angrier. And do the dogs break off the chase or game and return to their owner? Of course not. To all intents and purposes, they are totally deaf. This does not excuse you from teaching your deaf dog the recall signal, in fact it is essential.

There are two major components to teaching your dog to come back when 'called'

- Teach your dog to obey a recall hand signal.

- Teach your dog to pay attention to you.

I made two fundamental mistakes when teaching Lady the 'recall'. First, I let her off-lead too soon. I rather stupidly thought that she would want to stay with me because I'm a nice guy. (Honest, I am). I soon realised that there were more exciting and interesting things to explore and chase. When a puppy is just a few weeks old, he is more likely to want to stay with his owner because he lacks confidence with the outside world. You must not get complacent during this time, because as he gets a little older and his confidence grows, he is more likely to want to run off and explore.

The second mistake I made was that I had not perfected my 'recall' signal, so although she could see me gesticulating towards her, she didn't pay any attention to me. So it was back to the drawing board and after a great deal of thought came up with the following criteria:

- I had to be more interesting than anything else we are likely to meet on our walks; other people, other dogs, horse riders, birds, a falling leaf, etc.

- I could not afford to ignore her and let her go off to do her own thing. She was with me and our walks were together, not as individuals.

- I needed to have perfected my recall signal so she obeyed it every time.

- When she returned to me, she must get lots of praise and a reward.

- Occasionally, I would put her on-lead and walk for a couple of minutes, and then I would let her off again. By doing this, she would not anticipate the end of the walk and her reward would be to go and play again.

Let's just examine a typical scenario of someone taking their dog for a walk. Owner and dog have arrived at the park and the dog is let off-lead. The dog is allowed to run off anywhere he likes while the owner ambles around the park totally ignoring his dog. The owner may be chatting to a friend or partner while they walk but has very little idea of what the dog is doing. At the end of the walk, the owner calls the dog to put him on-lead to go home.

The dog in the meantime is having a super time doing exactly what he likes. Perhaps he's annoying other dog walkers and their dogs or he's getting into a scrap or scaring children. Maybe he's picked up the scent of wildlife and gone on a chase. He hears his owner calling his name but he's learnt that that is a signal for going home and he's not ready yet. So he ignores his owner. Eventually, after much fuss and chasing, the owner catches his dog, struggles to put the lead on and finally goes home.

This scenario may be a little exaggerated but I'm sure most of us have experienced some, if not all, of those problems. With a deaf dog, you cannot afford to allow your dog to do any of those things.

Through my experiences with Lady I have devised a training programme that has been carried out by several of my clients with great success. It is not a quick-fix and will therefore take time to teach. The emphasis is on interacting with your dog, and paying him attention so you are the one he wants to be with.

The first piece of advice I give to my clients when teaching the recall signal, is to make the most of every opportunity that presents itself For example, if you are sitting watching television and your dog wanders up to you, don't ignore him or take him for granted. As he's walking towards you, reinforce what he's doing by giving your recall signal so he begins to associate what he's doing with your signal.

The second piece of advice is to consider what signal to use. Remember the dog will eventually be some distance from you so it needs to be a signal he can clearly see. I use an open arm waving motion. Two arms are twice as good! If your dog is quite far away, sway your body. A moving target is easier to see.

I start the teaching process by just sitting in the lounge and throwing a piece of food across the room. Make sure your puppy sees it and no doubt he'll go and eat it. Once he realises that you are the source of the food, he is likely to come back to you for more. As he does so, give your recall signal. This is starting the association of the signal with coming to you. When he gets to you, get him to sit, and then throw another piece of food across the room. Repeat the process at intervals until you think your puppy understands the command. It's even a good way to feed your puppy – providing you feed dry kibble!

When you think puppy has understood what the signal means then take the next step. Move into the garden and have the puppy run between two people. They are both crouched down (remember your body language. If you bend over your puppy you might intimidate him so crouch down) and both are holding titbits. Using the titbits, encourage the puppy to run between each person and the person he's running towards gives the recall signal and smiles when he's going in the right direction. When he arrives, he gets the titbit and lots of fuss, and the person has an absolutely delighted facial expression.

You can then progress to the next stage. Walk the puppy around the back garden on an extendible lead or a reasonably long line. You should have with you whatever your dog really likes. Ideally this would be his favourite toy like a ball, and you should plan to take this with you on walks when the time comes. Have the extendible lead free-running so there is no tension on it and allow your puppy to do whatever puppies do in the garden, sniff, urinate, dig holes, cut the grass, whatever. (See figure 14). After a few seconds walk into your puppy's line of vision and attract his attention with his favourite toy. As he comes towards you give the recall signal and smile. (See figures 15 and 16). When he gets right up to you, throw the toy for him as a reward.

There are two things to keep in mind during this exercise:

1. The extendable lead should be free-running at all times and at no time should you take up the tension to influence what your puppy does. All his actions should be voluntary. The only reason the lead is attached is just in case he decides to go on a walk-about.

2. The reward of the toy should only be given when your puppy arrives right up to you. Many people make the mistake of rewarding their puppy by throwing the toy when he is on his way back but is still some distance away from his owner. The object of the exercise is to teach the dog to return to the owner, not to return part of the way. The reward should therefore only be given when the dog has done what the owner has asked of him.

Figure 14. Allow your puppy to wander

Figure 15. Attract your puppy's attention and give the 'recall' signal

Figure 16. Reward the recall with a game or food treat

You should find after a few repetitions, your puppy starts to get the hang of it and will voluntarily look to you to ask if the toy is coming out. The answer is a quite categorically 'YES', because that is exactly what you want from your puppy. You want him to look to you. You want him to pay you attention. This is what you are teaching him, so if he voluntarily looks to you, give him the recall signal, smile, and when he gets to you reward him with the toy.

Having made some progress, you can then move to somewhere unfamiliar to your puppy, like a friend or neighbour's garden. The new place should not have too many distractions although there will of course be different sights and smells. The whole process of attracting your pup's attention, recalling and rewarding him is repeated. During this process, he is still on the extendible lead.

When you feel you are getting the desired response from your puppy, you can move to the park during a quiet part of the day when there are not too many dogs or people. Remember your puppy is still on the extendible lead as you go through the whole training process again. Continue going to the park, and as your puppy becomes more proficient at paying you attention and coming when 'called', build in more and more distractions by going at busier times. Eventually you can go to the park at prime dog walking time and your puppy only has eyes for you because you are the one that's fun to be with.

Having reached this stage, you can then return to your back garden and repeat the whole training programme again, but this time your dog is off-lead. Only move from one stage to another as your puppy becomes more proficient at paying you attention and coming when 'called'.

You may want to use two or three regular walks so if your puppy does wander off and you lose him, at least he will be on familiar ground and hopefully, will make his way back home or to the car. If you just plod around the same walks day after day, you are going to become rather boring to your puppy and he will wander off to find his own amusement. So as well as playing with your puppy, try to vary your routes and change direction frequently. This will keep him guessing as to where you are going which will help to keep his attention.

Don't overlook the need for an ID disc on your puppy's collar. It is a legal requirement and it also makes common sense.

WALKING ON A LOOSE LEAD

I've called this section 'Walking on a Loose Lead' because that's what most dog owners want. Unless you are intending to participate in obedience competitions, then there is no need to have the dog 'glued' to your left leg; he only needs to walk nicely by your side without pulling. Conventionally, a dog is usually taught to walk on his owners left side. It doesn't really matter which side your puppy walks as long as you are consistent to begin with. Later, when your puppy learns the signal for 'nice walking' you can teach him to walk on either side. To start this exercise you do not need your puppy on-lead. What, no lead? No choke chain? There is absolutely no need to use a choke chain, regardless of the breed of dog or whether he can hear or not. If owners take the time and trouble to train their puppy properly in the first place, choke chains would become extinct!

There are two stages to teaching your puppy to walk nicely at your side.

1. Start by teaching your puppy to walk on your left. Place the food treat in the palm of your left hand and hold it in place with your thumb. Position your left hand by your left knee so the puppy's nose, following the treat, is in line with your knee, (Figure 17). This may mean you are bent double, particularly if you have a small breed of dog! Walk around the garden and your puppy should follow your hand with the treat. You must keep your hand by your leg as that is where you want your puppy to walk. The purpose of this exercise, apart from teaching you that you don't have to pull the dog around on a lead, is to get him used to following you and introducing him gradually to what the 'nice walking' signal will be; an open hand, arm straight down and a little way out

Figure 17. Lure puppy off-lead

from the side of your body. If he starts to wander off, get his attention back by placing the titbit under his nose. Only take three or four steps to begin with, then stop and reward your puppy, providing he has been walking correctly at your side.

2. The next step is called targeting. We want your puppy to 'target' your left hand by touching it with his nose. Once your puppy is used to you having food treats in your left hand, remove them to the right hand. Hold your left hand, arm and fingers extended downwards by your left side, and as soon as your puppy looks at your left hand, stop and reward him with a food treat from the right hand. Repeat this procedure for a few times. Now put a little bit of pressure on him by ignoring the looking at the hand and waiting until a he gets a little closer to the hand, then stop and reward him. The final step of targeting is to get the puppy to actually touch the hand, then bingo, lots of praise and food treats.

3. When your puppy happily follows you, you can put him on-lead. This is the time when a lot of owners teach their puppy to pull so, YOU MUST KEEP A LOOSE LEAD. Imagine someone tugging at the back of your collar. Your natural reaction is to counter that action by going forward, otherwise you will fall over! This is what we teach our pups when we keep a tight lead, as their natural reaction is to counter our pulling backwards by pulling forward. The training procedure is the same as without the lead but now you are to standing up straight and using the left hand as the target and the signal for 'loose lead walking'. If your puppy starts to go off in another direction, get his attention with the titbit and bring him back to your side. Change direction often so he keeps an eye on you. Always use the 'loose lead walking' signal when he is walking by your side and reward frequently. (Figure 18).

Figure 18. Final 'loose lead walking' signal

If your puppy starts to jump up for the treat, stop, and remove it to the right hand and take it out of reach. Do not continue with the 'loose lead walking' exercise until he has stopped jumping up. Keep your left hand in the 'loose lead walking' position all the time your puppy is walking nicely at your side but as soon as he loses interest or starts to wander bring the titbit back to the left hand and get his attention with it until he is back in the 'loose lead walking' position.

Despite early training with titbits, some puppies will insist on pulling on the lead. If you experience difficulties with your puppy walking on a loose lead, there are two other courses of action open to you:

1) As your puppy pulls ahead, watch the lead. Just when it is about to become tight, stop; even walk backwards until your dog realises he's not moving forward. He'll probably come back to your side on his own but if not encourage him back to your side with a titbit, praise him, change direction and start again. To your puppy, to carry on walking when he is pulling is perceived as a reward and he must not be rewarded for pulling, only when the lead is loose. It is important that you do stop when the lead goes tight and you don't move until your puppy is back at your side.

2) Despite the best efforts of some owners, some dogs will insist on pulling. Perhaps there is more than one dog in the family and the dogs are pulling to get ahead of each other, or perhaps the dog is so keen to get to the park for a walk. For these dogs, try a head collar like the Gentle Leader or Haiti.

STAY

For this exercise I would not recommend using titbits as your puppy will probably want to come to you for the food treat. At this stage it doesn't matter if your puppy is laying down, standing or sitting; all you are doing is getting him used to the signal to 'stay'. (Later, you can combine exercises to practise sit/stay, down/stay or stand/stay.) Obviously your puppy will need to be looking at you, so stand directly in front of him with his lead on and give the 'stay' hand signal; an arm raised like you are taking the oath in court, (Figure 19). Keep your hand in the 'stay' position and stand in front of your puppy for a few seconds, then praise him and release him from the 'stay'. All the time he is staying, say 'good dog' so your face has a happy, smiling expression. If he starts to wander off or move around, have a blank, emotionless facial expression, put him back in position and start again.

Figure 19. Stand in front of your puppy

When your puppy will stay for a few seconds with you standing in front of him, take one step backwards, still with your arm in the 'stay' position, and directly return to your puppy and praise him. Repeat this exercise but wait for two seconds before returning to him. Then take two steps backwards and gradually, step by step, increase the distance and the time you ask him to 'stay', until you are at the end of the lead. At this stage your hand signal will vary slightly. Your arm will be outstretched in front of you with your hand held upwards in much the same way as a policeman stopping traffic, (Figure 20). If he wanders off, put him back in position without rewarding him and start again. At the end of each successful 'stay', return to your puppy keep the 'stay' hand signal in place, reward and praise him. When you reach the end of the lead, have someone else hold it, or tie the end to a gate post and repeat the same procedure. You can also start to gradually increase the time for him to stay, but don't try too much too soon as you don't want him to fail. Don't forget to smile at your puppy and tell him he's a good dog all the while he is staying. If he wanders off, immediately change to a blank, emotionless facial expression.

Figure 20. Gradually move backwards

I must stress that this is a very gradual process and must not be hurried. Only increase the distance between you and your puppy as he succeeds at each distance. When he becomes adept at staying, vary the time and distance so he doesn't start to anticipate your next command.

10 HOUSETRAINING

The principles for housetraining a deaf dog are very much the same as housetraining a hearing dog. Housetraining relies on timing and vigilance - *your* timing and *your* vigilance. This is where you start using the 'praise' body posture I mentioned earlier. When you first get your puppy home, take him into the garden where you would ordinarily want him to eliminate. When he obliges, smile and give a 'good dog' hand signal and reward with a food treat, a stroke or a cuddle.

There are key times when a puppy will need to eliminate;

- When he's woken up
- Shortly after his meal
- After a period of excitement or play

In addition you need to be aware of the last time your puppy eliminated so you need to take him outside at regular intervals, say every 30 minutes to one hour. Don't just open the door and let him out; go with him so you are in a position to praise him when he obliges. Don't attempt to play or any form of interaction while your puppy is thinking about what he's out there to do. Just stay still and watch. As your puppy starts to get the idea that outdoors is where he is supposed to eliminate you can start to develop a signal that means 'go pee'. There is of course only so long you can hang around the back garden waiting for your puppy to produce. If it seems that he isn't going to eliminate then bring him back indoors and keep him with you. Do not allow him to run around the house or he'll probably eliminate somewhere indoors. This is where an indoor kennel, or crate, comes in handy once the puppy has been acclimatised to it. If your puppy doesn't feel the need to eliminate, bring him indoors and place him in the crate. After about 20 minutes, take him outside again and repeat the procedure until he has eliminated outside. And *praise* him using facial expression, body posture food treats, strokes and cuddles.

Housetraining should continue 24 hours a day so what happens at night? Well, you can have the puppy in his basket or crate in your bedroom and when he becomes restless, take him outside (yes I know it will be dark and the middle of the night so get the old man to do it!). You can fit a bell to the pup's collar which may help you rouse from your night's slumber. Alternatively you can leave the pup where he would usually sleep, probably the kitchen, and use a baby listener for any sound of movement. I appreciate this will be inconvenient for a short while but ultimately it makes the housetraining process quicker. Also if you don't make the effort to take your puppy outside during the night, it could send mixed signals to your puppy; during the day it is not the done thing to eliminate indoors, but during the night it's OK.

The method of housetraining by spreading newspaper all over a room is gradually being replaced by the more vigilant approach to housetraining. The basis being that the more times the puppy has of getting it wrong (eliminating indoors) the longer it will take to get it right (eliminating outdoors).

There will of course be times when your puppy will have an accident and produce something on your carpet that you would have preferred him not to have done. On such occasions there is nothing you can do except clean it up. It was your fault the accident happened as you weren't being sufficiently vigilant. If you come home from shopping and find a 'mess' on the carpet, just clean it up. Do not draw your pup's attention to it or reprimand him in any way. A reprimand, or praise, must come within one second of the action so the dog will associate the praise or reprimand with what he's done, so if you reprimand pup for 'messing' on the carpet while you are out, he will not realise why he is being reprimanded. No good will come from rubbing your pup's nose in the mess which is an old fashioned, disgusting wives-tale. It's totally unnecessary, yet people still do it. No good will come from showing your displeasure or inflicting any form of reprimand as this will only teach your puppy that if he needs to eliminate and you haven't seen the signals, then he will go and hide from you to do his 'business' - and he may even eat the evidence.

If you see your puppy is about to eliminate indoors, the signs to watch for are sniffing or circling on a spot he may have used before, or general restlessness. If you catch pup just about to eliminate, you can't get his attention by shouting at him so you need some other way of getting his attention, and quickly. Therefore during the housetraining period I suggest you carry something you can throw into your puppy's line of vision. A piece of cloth the size of a handkerchief for example tied with several knots. These can fit either into your pocket or tucked under your trouser belt. Having got your puppy's attention, pick him up and take him outside.

11 UNWANTED BEHAVIOUR

Many people wrongly attribute unwanted behaviour from their deaf puppy or dog on the fact that he is deaf. However, in many instances, it's the owner that has encouraged the behaviour when the dog was still a puppy, or the puppy hasn't been trained or socialised properly. Therefore, do not encourage behaviour in a puppy that you would not want in an adult dog.

There are a number of common behavioural problems that some owners find difficult to cope with. Here's how to prevent three of the most common problems;

JUMPING UP

When we get our new puppy home, it's really sweet when he jumps up on our leg and his paws only reach our kneecaps. We smile and stroke him or pick him up. Already the puppy has learnt that if he jumps up, he gets attention. The situation is not helped when you invite friends round to see your new puppy and they also pick him up and within a short period of time he has learnt that anyone is fair game to be jumped on.

The answer to this problem is simple; don't let it become a problem by encouraging jumping up in the first place. When your puppy jumps up, totally ignore him. Do not look at him or touch him (and with a hearing dog, don't speak to him either). You don't see dogs jumping up at inanimate objects like a telegraph pole, or a lamp-post for attention, so that's what you must become - an inanimate object. Your puppy may jump up even more to begin with because he's trying that much harder to get your attention. But stick with it, as when he realises there is no reward for jumping up, he will gradually stop. You must also tell visitors to your home not to pay any attention to your puppy until he is sitting.

BARKING

Dogs will bark for many reasons but one of the most common reasons is to get his owners attention. Various methods owners try to stop their dog barking are; to soothe and stroke him; try to hold his mouth shut; hit the dog, (and with a hearing dog, to talk or shout at him). None of these methods work. In fact they all encourage the dog to bark more because in all cases the dog achieves his object, he gets his owners attention, even if it is in a form of a reprimand.

If your puppy is barking to get your attention, ignore it. Don't look at him or touch him. Better still, walk away from your puppy so the barking has the opposite effect to what he is trying to achieve. When he realises his behaviour is not reaping any rewards, he will gradually stop. If he is barking for another reason, interrupt it by getting his attention with a toy or food treat then direct his attention to something you would prefer him to do.

HOME ALONE

Dogs are social animals and it is unnatural for them to be on their own for long periods of time. However, there will of course be times when a dog needs to be left on his own for an hour or two while the family go out. Many dogs do not like being left even for this short time as they are used to having company virtually 24 hours a day, so they find isolation difficult to cope with. From the time you get your puppy home, start to acclimatise him to spending short periods on his own. Put him in the kitchen with a chew toy to occupy him, and after one minute, if he's quiet, let him out. Do not go back to him if he's barking or whining because this will teach him that 'I bark and somebody comes'. If he does bark, then next time you put him in the kitchen, it should only be for a few seconds.

Very gradually extend the time you leave your puppy so he eventually becomes accustomed to being left on his own. Do not make a fuss of him when you leave him or when you return. Be very matter-of fact about your departure and your return.

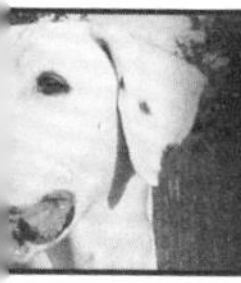

12 NOW WHAT?

You now have the basic hand signals for praise, reprimand, sit, down, stand, walking on a loose lead, stay, and come back. So what now? Well this depends how adventurous and confident you feel. For example while walking your puppy on-lead you can use the lead to communicate what you want him to do. Taking up the tension means stop, one slight tug on the lead means, sit.

Over the years the communication with Lady has become quite subtle. A slight movement of the fingers, a wave of the hand, a facial expression can all communicate a message or command. You can use all sorts of hand and arm signals to teach your puppy to do the same things hearing dogs are trained to do. For example;

Lady knows a signal for waiting in the car until I 'tell' her she can come out.

When she is off-lead on a walk and we come to a where the path divides, I indicate the way we will be going by pointing in that direction, and off she goes.

Occasionally, when I'm throwing the ball for Lady, it ends up lost in long grass or bushes. A shrug of my shoulders and arms out-stretched means, 'find the ball'.

She knows that when we get home from our walk, she doesn't go running through the house covered in mud, she goes to the kitchen to have her paws wiped.

A waggle of my fingers mean, 'fetch a toy and I'll play with you'.

What you can achieve is limited only by your imagination and dedication. I'm sure I could have achieved more with Lady if I had been more imaginative!

Finally, the prospect of training a deaf puppy may seem daunting to begin with and will probably put many people off because of the challenges they will face. There are a lot of good words used to describe training a puppy; perseverance, patience, commitment, time and dedication to name but a few. Multiply these several times over and you have an idea of what is involved in training a deaf puppy. There are no quick-fixes, short-cuts or magic formulae. However, it is possible to train a deaf puppy given the right environment and the right training methods. Eventually your efforts will reap their own rewards and you will be able to enjoy your relationship with your puppy to the full.

Figure 20. Lady behaving like a 'normal' dog

ASSOCIATION OF PET DOG TRAINERS (APDT)

Addresses

UK
PO Box 17
Fairford
Gloucester
GL7 4WZ
www.apdt.co.uk

USA
1507 21st Street
Ste.204
Sacramanto
CA 95814
www.apdt.com

NOTES